About the author

Stephanie Schmid has had a diverse and successful career spanning over 30 years. She spent the majority of her career at ADP, leading teams and providing insights and solutions for clients in the Human Resources field. She has led teams and directed relationships with large, **Fortune 500 companies**. She worked in the technology sector for **Vivint Smart Home** and as a leader on **eBay's Global People Team**.

Stephanie has a reputation for driving results, building relationships, and leading high-performing teams. She has mentored and coached numerous teams and individuals.

Understanding the complexities of leadership, the intricate dynamics of corporate politics, and the delicate balance between personal and professional spheres, Stephanie's coaching style is rooted in empathy, compassion, and tangible results. *Building trust and creating a safe space for vulnerability and growth are at the core of her coaching process.*

Stephanie feels passionate about *giving back* to the community and *volunteered for* various youth sports teams, professional organizations, and within her church. When she isn't at work or volunteering, you can find her *running, biking, swimming, hiking, scuba diving, playing pickleball or spending time with family. She loves travelling to new places, experiencing different cultures, and continually learning and* increasing her understanding of individuals.

What will you find in the next pages?

- Inspiring thoughts from Stephanie's personal and professional life
- Motivational advice and prompts for a more positive life
- Important questions, to make you think and make real change
- Insightful learning from inspirational people we all admire

Your mindset, a powerful tool within your grasp, is the cornerstone of your journey. Delve into these stories to nurture a positive mindset and gain a new perspective on life. This collection serves as a gentle nudge to keep your mind open and cultivate an optimistic attitude. Your mindset is the compass guiding your experiences, and this book will help you set it firmly in the direction of positivity.

This collection of simple stories and quotes with a big impact will undoubtedly bring you a more positive outlook on life. It's a treasure trove of wisdom and inspiration, meticulously curated to guide you towards conquering your limitations and transforming your dreams into a vibrant reality.

Stephanie, the heart and mind behind these remarkable words, generously shares her personal experiences, offering you a glimpse into a life lived to the fullest.

This collection is a potent reminder of the strength of the human spirit and the boundless potential within each of us. It's a lifeline for those moments when life feels challenging and uncertain, offering guidance, comfort, and the assurance that with the right mindset and determination, we can surmount any obstacle.

Open when you feel like you want a sprinkle of inspiration!

en-thu-si-asm: intense and eager enjoyment, interest, or approval.

Just the word "enthusiasm" brings a smile to my face. *What are you enthusiastic about?* As you encounter things that are daunting or challenging – identify something that sparks your enthusiasm.

Your enthusiasm will make a difference in your interactions with others and will add energy to your day.

Hearing children laughing is not only a beautiful sound but never ceases to bring a smile to my face. Research has shown that children laugh an average of 300-400 times a day while adults typically laugh only 15 times per day.

The health benefits of laughter include: *pain relief, increased happiness, and increased immunity.*

Can we find something to be grateful for when the world is at its worst?

My heart goes out to people struggling. You or someone you love might be struggling. People are without heat, water, and basic supplies. Lives are being lost and homes destroyed.

Through all of the devastation, however, I am impressed to hear stories of gratitude coming from impacted individuals. Gratitude for family members, friends, kindness, food, and the generosity of strangers.

It was a great reminder to me of the numerous things I often don't take time to appreciate. If we want to have joy and happiness, the first step is to identify our gratitude. Regardless of the challenges we face, there is ALWAYS something to be grateful for.

What are you grateful for?

My core belief is that people are usually doing the best they can.

Putting that into action is sometimes challenging when you have expectations for people to behave a certain way based on past interactions or presumptions.

If you are disappointed because you feel someone has let you down, I would encourage you to reflect on why you feel this way and if that disappointment is based on the expectations you have placed on that individual.

Reframe your disappointment through a lens of seeing them as someone doing the best that they can. I know when I choose to do this, it is actually ME who benefits most because I no longer assume negative intentions, but can rather focus on an individual's strengths and positive intentions.

We all benefit when we generously give people the benefit of the doubt and eliminate our own expectations of how we want them to behave.

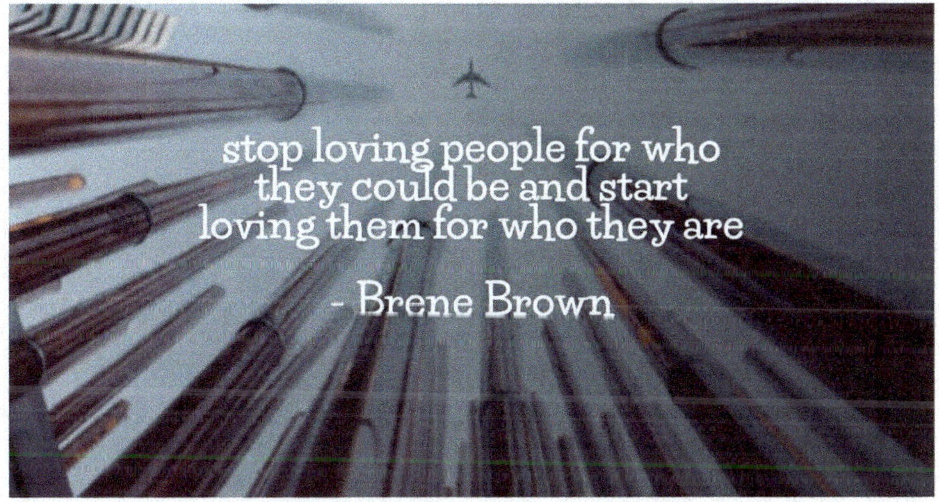

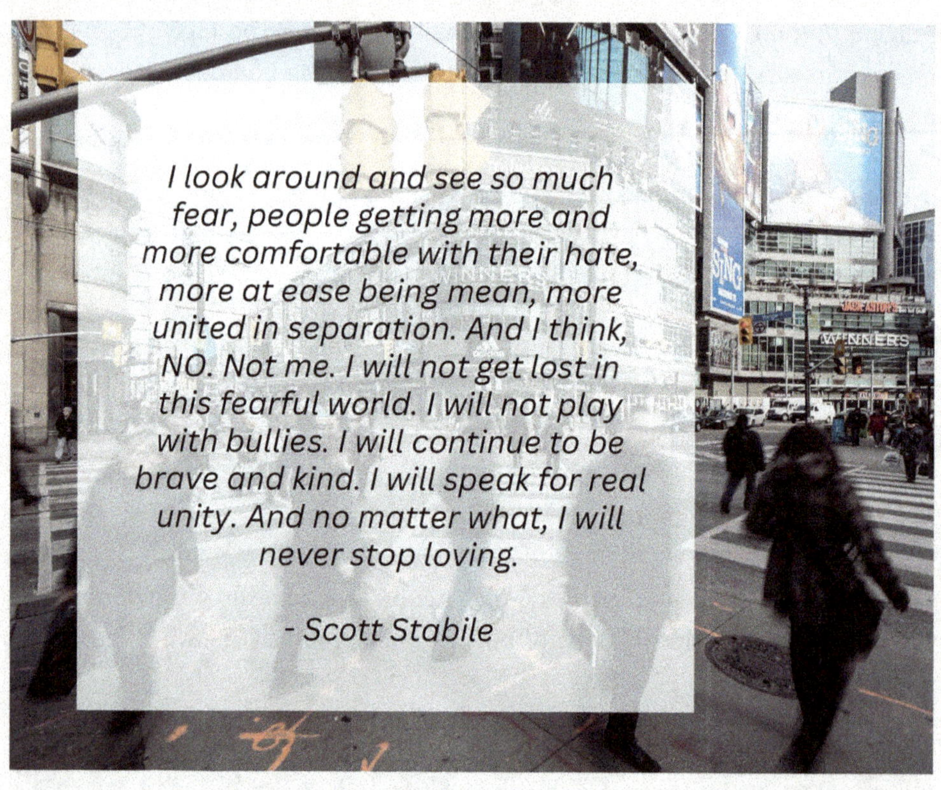

We can all listen more and strive to understand more. Our diversity and different experiences can give us greater compassion and understanding. You don't need to agree with someone in order to understand them. Each person matters as well as their opinion. Try to truly understand someone else's perspective.

Every day we face challenges.

It is very easy to be frustrated, disappointed, and even angry when things don't go the way we plan or expect.

In each of those situations, however, there is something to be grateful for. Regardless of what has happened in your past – you are not your past.

Today is a new opportunity to look for the good and find something to be grateful for in each situation and interaction.

You choose your outlook – recognize the good in your life today!

Turn your "I won't" challenge into an "I will" opportunity

The more we think about something, the more we reinforce those thoughts in our minds.

Ironic process theory or ironic rebound refers to the psychological process whereby deliberate attempts to suppress certain thoughts make them more likely to surface. **We all have something we want to stop doing.** Instead of focusing on what you "won't" do, redefine your challenge as something you "will" do. For example, instead of telling yourself "I won't let the meeting go over time", tell yourself, "I will end this meeting 2 minutes early". Select one of your "I won't" challenges this week and flip it to an "I will" opportunity and see what difference it makes for you!

When you are feeling helpless, REMEMBER that you have gone through difficulties. REMEMBER that you have made a difference in other people's lives.

REMEMBER that you have been kind and have cared for and helped others. REMEMBER that you have skills, abilities and experience that make you uniquely you. Just as you have made a difference in the past, you can make a difference now. ***Focus on what you CAN do instead of focusing on things over which you have no control.***

How do you view stress? Most of us likely try to avoid it or figure out how to best manage it.

I love Kelly McGonigal's insight as she encourages us to rethink our relationship with stress. *Stress will only kill you if you THINK it will.*

I am continually impressed with the power of our minds and the messages we reinforce for ourselves. Kelly says, *"Really the best way to make decisions is to go after what it is that creates meaning in your life, and then trust yourself to handle the stress that follows."* You have more power than you think you do. Reframe stress as your friend–as a cheerleader who helps push you forward.

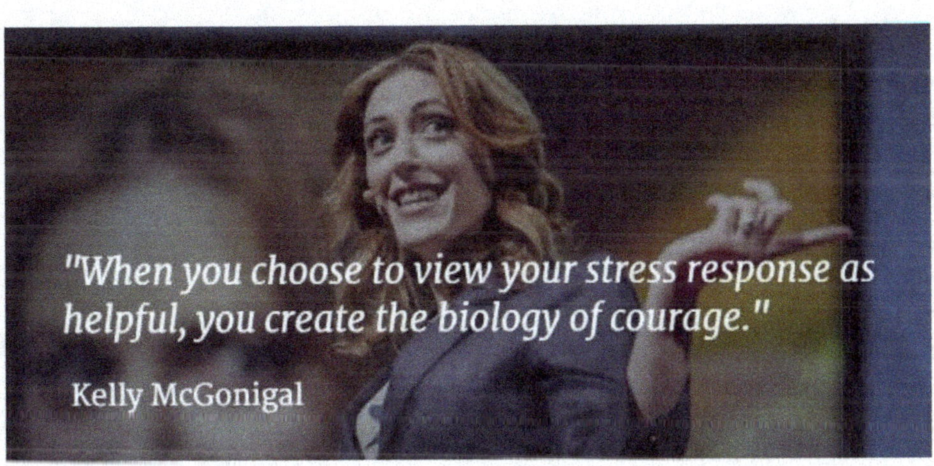

Our expectations are often
altered by things outside of
our control.
If we pin our happiness on those
expectations, we will be
disappointed and discouraged.
Expectations of others work
the same way – the behavior
of other people is not something
we can control.

**Instead of focusing on expectations,
focus on being grateful for things that do happen.**
Gratitude brings peace and appreciation for your situation instead of resentment for unmet expectations.

The incredible Barbara Corcoran teaches us about fostering **energy, diligence, faith, and grit** whenever things get difficult. Instead of discouragement, we can dig deep and find the opportunity in any setback.

Focus on the possibilities!

I am so grateful for all those who have served and sacrificed for our freedoms.

Jennie Taylor is the widow of the late Brent Taylor who died in 2018 in the service of his country. In a podcast I listened to, she said, *"...the best way to honor them is to take the lives we've been given and do something honorable."*

We might have family members or know someone who has given the ultimate sacrifice. Each of us can make a difference by how we treat others and how we use our unique selves to make a difference–even if it is small difference–every day.

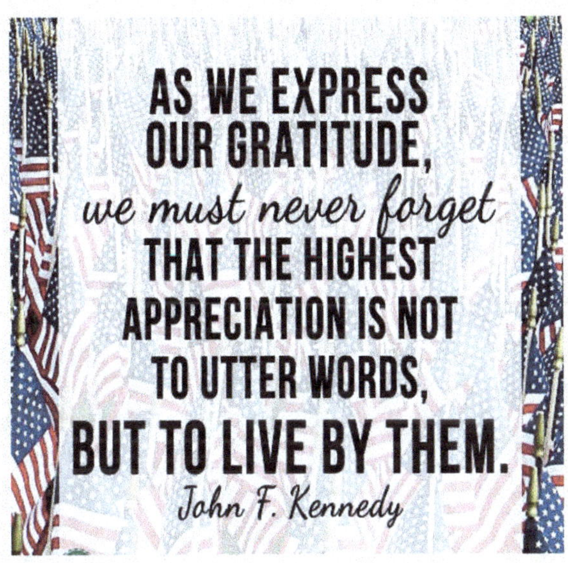

Our stress and anxiety are understandable, especially at times of uncertainty. If instead, however, we *CHOOSE* to use this unsettling and upsetting time to focus on gratitude, we will feel a measure of peace. For the benefit of your mental health and well-being and those around you, take time each day this week to write down and share what you are grateful for.

With many things not in our control – it is important to focus on controlling the things within the span of our individual influence. ***You can control your attitude and your mindset. You can control how you treat others.***

I would encourage you to also control how you start each day. Start each day with a ***routine*** that includes some exercise (getting outside is great!), shower, getting dressed and going into an area that you designate for work.

Creating a routine will help you be more productive and will give you more grounding. Choose not to stay in your PJs all day or work at the kitchen table where everyone is going in and out, interrupting your focus. You have resilience and adaptability in your DNA – you can make a positive impact in this time of volatility.

We can spend a lot of time frustrated, angry, or agonizing over things that we cannot control. **Focus on the things you can control.** Choose to see the positive and good instead of focusing on the negative in your situation.

Choose to dance to whatever music is played.

Feeling frazzled? Overwhelmed by your many commitments?

Our 'to do' lists are typically long and contain more items than we can ever complete in the time available. This causes stress, burnout, and more painfully, lost opportunities with our family and friends as we often prioritize work over all else.

I find that taking a 'break' through meditation, a quick walk, or a chat with family/friends helps ground me and supports my desire to put things in proper perspective. I had the opportunity to see Howard Jones and loved his reminder that we don't need to treat everything with such urgency. ***Take a little time today for perspective.***

———————————————————

Here's a story as an inspiration to not give up…

The Wave in Coyote Buttes North on the Utah/Arizona border is a beautiful natural wonder of red sandstone rock. In order to comply with the Wilderness Act and preserve the fragile nature of the foundation, the BLM only allows 20 people to hike The Wave each day.

Half of the permits are granted through an online lottery and the other half are granted at an in-person lottery. We have participated in both lotteries for several years to no avail. I had given up on the possibility of hiking The Wave. Unbeknownst to me, my husband had not given up.

He entered the online lottery and specifically selected a less popular month and day when there were fewer requests to increase his likelihood of success. And he was selected!! The Wave was a surreal experience. We only had the opportunity to hike The Wave because my husband considered other possibilities (time of year and day) and kept trying for the permit.

Don't give up – be creative in your approach; your next effort may be the one that is successful!

Embrace and magnify your strengths and talents.
You are in control of yourself.
You choose how you react to the situations and circumstances around you.

———————————————————

Instead of spending energy focusing on finding fault with products, processes, or people, focus on what you can contribute to the solution. How you frame your challenges and opportunities matters! Perceive the best intent in others instead of blaming others. **Focus on your strengths and what you can add to situations you encounter.**

"Your worst enemy cannot harm you as much as your unguarded thoughts" – Buddha.

What you think about matters. Think positive, productive thoughts.

I love the movie *"About Time."* It shares a powerful, positive message that we can find joy every day. Even though work and life have challenges and stress, you can find something in every experience and every opportunity that is good and positive. **You can choose joy when you focus on the positive!**

Your mind is powerful and thinks thousands of thoughts every day. Don't waste those thoughts in a state of anxiety about actual or potential problems. Instead **focus on what you can do today** and the things over which you have control. The future will happen whether you worry about it or not – so spend your time, thoughts and energy focused on what you can impact today.

Find something that is going great today. *Can you find at least one small thing?* Focus on it and the positive view will expand. This will improve your attitude and outlook and you will notice and attract more success!

Optimist:

Someone who figures that taking a step backward after taking a step forward is not a disaster, it's a cha-cha.

–Robert Brault

I love this definition of an optimist! Setbacks in our personal and professional lives might initially feel like disasters – but when we look and discover the positive aspects, backward steps are truly just an opportunity to dance a different way. Recognize the cha-cha step!

For most people, the swim portion is the least attractive element of a triathlon. As for me, I swim every week at a gym – I can see the lap lanes through my goggles in my lane. In the Spudman Triathlon however, I was swimming in murky water in a wide river & the only good my googles did was keep water out of my eyes. My wetsuit seemed confining & people bumped into me continually. I had to breathe deeply to shut down the automatic response to get anxious & stressed.

As you enter a new week or a new challenge, it may seem like you are in the swim portion of an open water triathlon when you've previously been swimming in a pool. There is murky water and lots of people who will bump into you as they also try to be successful. **You have the expertise and experience to work through this week's challenges – your experiences and training have prepared you to face something different than what you've done before. Remain calm.**

Keep moving forward and regularly check your bearings to make sure you don't need to adjust your angle. The swim portion is just a part of the race. Don't let it overwhelm you. It will eventually be done and you'll be ready for the next challenge with its own obstacles and rewards.

We all know that happiness doesn't come from things. Beyond finding happiness in our experiences and our relationships, however, happiness is something we can control through our thoughts.

Is your brain's natural path thinking negative thoughts?

Change your mindset and ask yourself these questions:
What am I grateful for right now?
How could I demonstrate excellence right now?
What can I control in my current situation?
Be mindful about what you are thinking about.

It's interesting how two people can be at the same event and have the same things happen to them and each person have a different experience. How we DECIDE to interpret our world makes a difference.

I love a quote from Deanna Murphy: "It's not what happens to you that causes your feelings, actions, and results. It's how you choose to see them that does."

Can you see stress and unrealistic deadlines/expectations as opportunities? Can you see the expertise and experience you are gaining as you struggle? Consciously, deliberately, and intentionally choose what you see – it will make a difference in your day and your life.

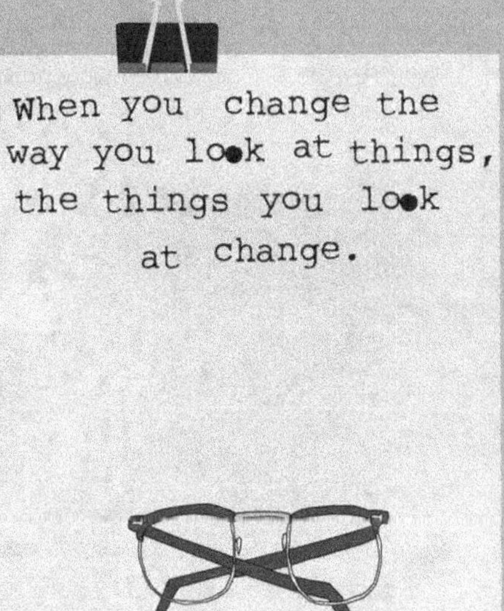

It is easy to be cynical and believe that other people are plotting against you. It is, however, a lot more beneficial for you to switch that attitude and begin with a belief that other people have the best intentions.

When I keep a mindset that everyone is doing the best they can, I am more understanding and kind when I interact with others. In my experience, beginning your interactions with others assuming the best intentions will improve your relationships and outlook on life.

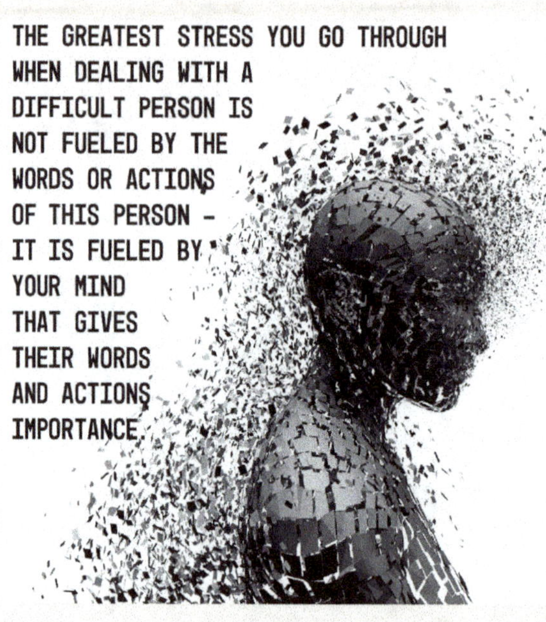

Dealing with difficult people is part of life. Don't let their negativity get you down.

Only your mind can give their words validity or importance. You own your perspective and can choose to not give any power to their comments. You are strong and powerful. Find the positive even when negative is spewed at you.

Things you can control:

1. Your beliefs
2. Your attitude
3. Your thoughts
4. Your perspective
5. How honest you are
6. Who your friends are
7. What books you read
8. How often you exercise
9. The type of food you eat
10. How many risks you take
11. How you interpret situations
12. How kind you are to others
13. How kind you are to yourself
14. How often you say "I love you"
15. How often you say "thank you"
16. How you express your feelings
17. Whether or not you ask for help
18. How often you practice gratitude
19. How many times you smile today
20. The amount of effort you put forth
21. How you spend/invest your money
22. How much time you spend worrying
23. How often you think about your past
24. Whether or not you judge other people
25. Whether or not you try again after a setback
26. How much you appreciate the things you have

It's easy to get concerned, worried or frustrated with things that happen in life. Even though there are many things outside of your control, there are many things directly IN YOUR CONTROL. If you feel anxious or that circumstances or life are unfair, I would encourage you to focus on what you can control.

Every day is filled with tiny miracles. Beyond the daily miracles of nature, if we pay attention, we will find miracles in everything. People who treat us with respect, appreciate our efforts, or are kind. Collaboration sessions that develop great ideas.

Tools and technology that work better than expected.
Creativity. New Ideas.
Meetings that end earlier than expected.
Exciting opportunities that are unexpected.
Food and Water.
Health and Stamina.
Autonomy.
Responsibility.
People who come into our lives just when needed.
Miracles abound.
Notice them. Appreciate them. Live grateful.

Your mind is so powerful.
You control how you perceive every situation.
When you have a negative thought – **replace it** with three positive thoughts and see how much better your life becomes. You are the driver of your life experience.

There are lots of challenges in life – focus on the things you can impact and don't waste your energy on things outside of your control.

I have always been someone who likes to be in control. I have had to learn over and over in my life that I can only control me. I cannot control other people or their reactions. I cannot control circumstances. I CAN, however, control my actions and my reactions. I control my attitude. I can work hard. I can make a difference in the lives of others – personally and professionally. My integrity, my passion and my focus matter. I may only be able to impact a small piece of a big puzzle – but I can make a difference every day. You can also make a difference today. Impact something you can control; do something YOU CAN DO!

There are many different approaches to leadership. I aspire to be the type of leader who shares and helps others find the positive in situations. I not only motivate myself when I find the positive but am also able to motivate others. In Skip Gilbert's book, *Keep Thinking – Thoughts for Success*, he shares **four great tips** for maintaining positive leadership:
1) Look for the good and we will see the good.
2) Look for others who believe as we do and partner with them to make a difference.
3) Make being a positive leader one of our goals.
4) Be consistent in our message.

I wholeheartedly embrace his conviction: *"In the end, being positive will produce superior results."* You have the power to find and share the positive.

> Being positive in a
> negative situation
> is not naive.
> It's
> *Leadership.*
>
> - Ralph Marston

5 Daily Reminders

1. I am amazing.
2. I can do anything.
3. Positivity is a choice.
4. I celebrate my individuality.
5. I am prepared to succeed.

Your thoughts proceed your actions. The messages you send yourself drive your attitude and the way you see the world.

When we radiate positivity and treat other people well, that outlook becomes a part of us. Scatter sunshine to others and have a great day.

Do you want to be happy?
Guess what – Happiness is in
your power!

You get to choose your
focus every day and how
you interpret your reality.
Life is made up of
challenges, problems and
pitfalls which you cannot
avoid. You can, however, see
challenges as opportunities
and face them with a
positive attitude. **Choose to
be a bit more happy today
than you were yesterday!**

When I began my undergraduate
studies many years ago, I had a
sign in my room reminding me to
"Enjoy the Journey."

That advice was helpful and
continues to be sound advice.
Obviously, we want to be
successful in our employment
and deliver quality in the process.
However – don't wait to be happy
until the end.

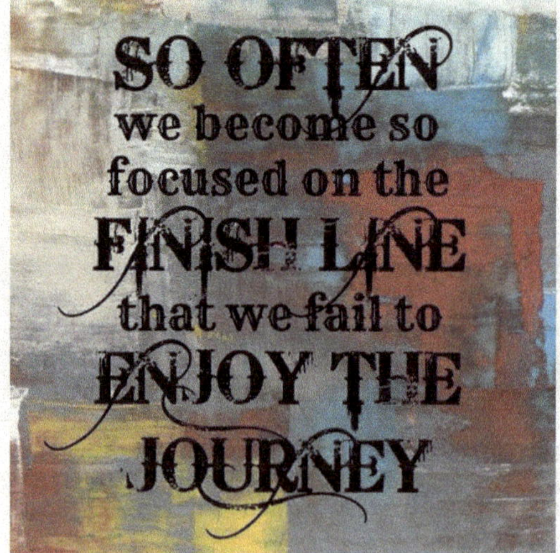

Did you notice how springtime shows us how some days include abundant sunshine and other days are cold and rainy (and even snowy)? Some days, you are surrounded by supporters; other days you meet detractors in every conversation. Most days have both ups and downs. The one thing we control is our own attitude. ***Bring your own sunshine to yourself and people you see!***

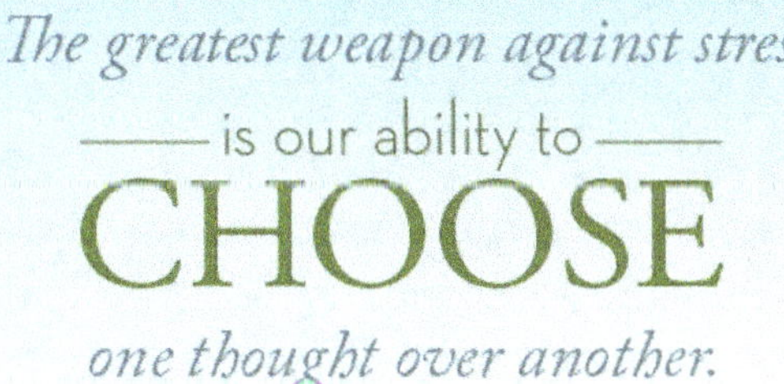

Stress is "a state of mental or emotional strain or tension resulting from adverse or very demanding circumstances." The competitive work environment is definitely demanding. Despite the intense pressures, your mind is MORE powerful.

You are strong and can CHOOSE how you deal with the pressures and demands of work.

You have the power within you to not allow the pressures to overpower you and to see the positive and the opportunities.

You control your mind and your mind is more powerful than the challenges you face.

- *Positive self-talk/affirmations*
- *Noticing your thoughts – counting positive ones!*
- *Meditation/prayer*
- *Music*
- *Exercise*
- *Taking breaks*
- *"Playing"/exploring/doing something new*
- *Listening or reading motivational messages every morning*
- *Volunteering – helping others*

The mind is everything.
what you think you become

- Buddha

I encourage you to select one of these ideas or any other idea to increase your positive thoughts. Make a conscious effort to increase your positivity.

What have you found works to help you increase your positivity?

Your mind is powerful – use it to increase your positivity and see the difference you can make!

We all love to be around positive, optimistic people!

Negativity drags us down and often makes us spiral into worse thoughts and feelings. While we all need a chance to vent – be selective in your venting. Once you've expressed the negative feelings, focus on the positive. When I distance myself from negativity, it has a huge impact on my outlook, my productivity and how I interact with others.

Be a positive force!

Who has helped you this week? What is going right with your mornings lately? Where are the positives in your day? Do you notice them?

It is amazing – the more you think about the good in your life, the more gratitude you'll feel. I challenge you to identify what you're grateful for today.

How do you view the last Monday in July?

With **dread and anxiety**? *("Summer is ending & the only sun exposure I get is from the light of my computer")*

Or do you visualize it with **excitement and full of prospects**? *("This is the last week of July–what a great opportunity to make a difference!")*

The week comes either way you look at it. The way you approach it, it will influence the quality of your work outputs and the nature of your interactions with others.

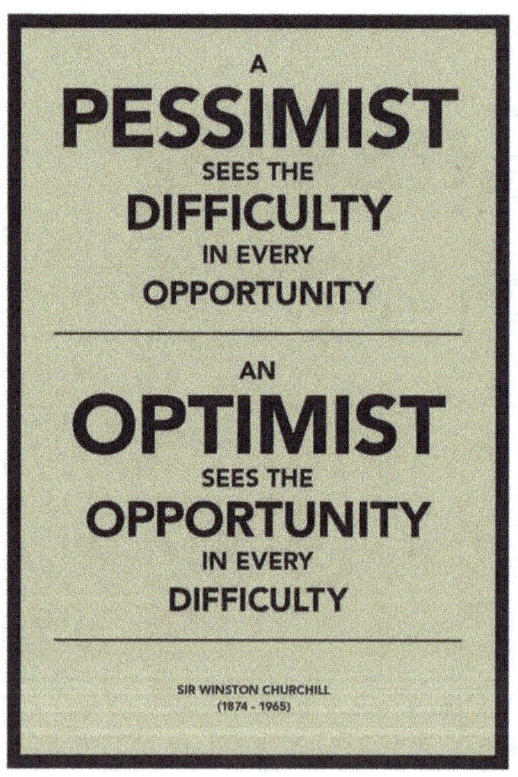

Crisp cold mornings, warm afternoons, and the beauty of leaves changing color are clear indications of autumn in Utah. Often, I find myself so focused on the destination that I fail to appreciate all the amazing things en route.

Even though there are a lot of obstacles and challenges, there is always something to appreciate in the midst of the storm.

Studies have shown, and my personal experience has validated, that making the effort and taking the time to be grateful truly increases your happiness.

What and who can you identify to be grateful for today?

When my children were young, my husband and I volunteered weekly to shelve books in their school library. I always preferred to do the shelving when no kids were in the library because I wanted to complete the task and leave the library with all the books neatly and correctly in place. **That, however, is not the point of a library! The books are there to be read, enjoyed, and support learning – not untouched and perfectly placed.**

We have similar recurring processes in our organizations and in our lives. Changing our mindset to accept that some things are recurring helps us change our definition of 'done' for those responsibilities.

How can you change your mindset this week around a recurring process? Where can you challenge yourself to consider new or different ways to see that ongoing event?

I have felt so much greater peace through this challenge as I have focused on all the incredible things and people I am grateful for, instead of being overwhelmed and distraught over all the things I cannot control.

Consciously choosing to be grateful and identifying things and people we are grateful for is a perspective shift that has a positive effect on our overall well-being. Regardless of the difficult things you are currently facing in your personal or professional life, **what can you be grateful for today?**

In the book *"Think Like a Monk"*, **Jay Shetty** shares the contrast between our natural "monkey mind' (which, like a monkey, jumps from branch to branch, never holding still) to a "monk mind". The monkey mind includes racing thoughts, worry, anxiety, difficulty focusing or being present.

The monk mind is calm, still, clear, and focused. Meditation, gratitude, mindfulness practices, and getting outside in nature are a few ways to begin cultivating a monk mind.

Do you feel the uncertainty of the daily life? Inflation, unemployment, AI replacing human interactions, unpredictable weather patterns...

When you face an environment of constant change, **are you viewing that uncertainty as a threat or as an opportunity?** Consciously identifying our mindset around change and choosing to shift that mindset, instead of allowing our automatic reaction to prevail, enables us to find opportunities instead of becoming paralyzed and discouraged.

It's a memorable day when I completed my **100th scuba dive,** BUT - at the end of that milestone dive, as I was climbing the ladder to the boat, I realized my dive camera was no longer on my wrist. Everyone joined in the underwater search for my memory keeper which contained images from the day's 3 three epic dives. I love pictures – they enable me to mentally return to experiences – to relive the events and associated emotions! Unfortunately, we were not successful in locating my camera and I don't have my underwater pictures from that day or my 100th dive.

...On the boat ride back, I had a choice to make: do I focus on what was lost or what was gained? I dove in a bucket list place in fantastic conditions (warm water, high visibility) with all my favorite dive buddies. Both things were true – the loss AND a fabulous, milestone experience. It was up to ME which to focus on.

You control your perspective. *This week, choose to focus on what you have gained instead of what you have lost.*

In the Schmicago series, there is a lovely song in the final episode which emphasizes that instead of focusing on 'happy endings' – we can look at every day as a 'happy beginning'.

Each day is a new opportunity to start fresh and try different strategies and methods.

Don't allow yesterday's challenges and disappointments to overshadow the new approach you can take today.

Instead of looking at the obstacles in your way or the disappointments, what can you celebrate in your life today?

Our minds are so powerful and keeping them healthy is even more critical than keeping our physical bodies healthy and strong. The word 'stress' has a powerful negative connotation and threatens our mental health.

We encounter stress daily – some outside of our control and some that we create. I find myself enlarging the things that cause me stress, making me more anxious than I was before thinking more about them. I have found that consciously slowing down my breathing (inhale for 4 counts, hold, exhale for 8 counts, hold, repeat), starting the day with meditation and prayer, and reframing the stress I can control as an 'opportunity' is so helpful. I have to remind myself that **stress, itself, isn't a negative thing.**

For things outside of my control, I do have control over my reactions and how I choose to internalize them. Instead of allowing stress to be debilitating, I can identify what actions I can take or what I need to let go.

THE CHOICE IS YOURS

It's a great time for us to embrace humor. <u>*Why not today?*</u> Studies have shown that a sense of humor can improve both your mental and physical health as well as improve your leadership skills. Instead of focusing on the disappointments and challenges you are facing, step back and find the humor in the situation.

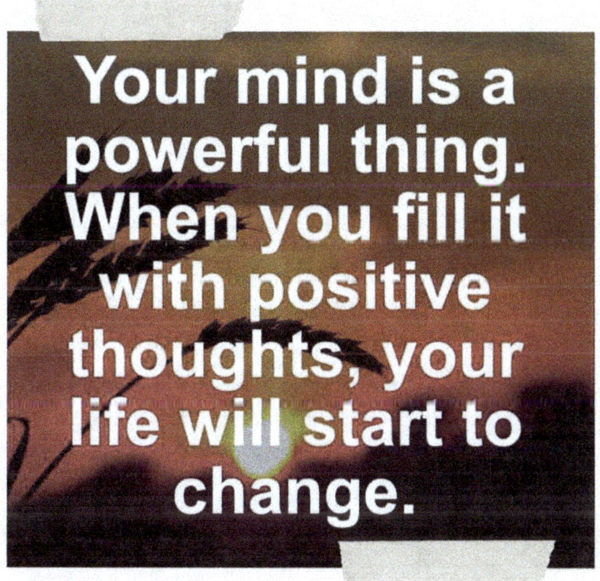

Have you ever noticed that when you tell yourself NOT to think about something, that 'thing' then becomes the focus of your thoughts? If this is your experience, you are not alone. *Ironic Process Theory* or *"The White Bear Phenomenon"* is the difficulty people have in suppressing a thought – **by trying not to think of something we find ourselves continually thinking of it**. So, this is a great week to flip the narrative and try your own experiment. Instead of thinking of something you "will not do" – find the opposite of that thing and tell yourself something you "will do" and see how that focus changes your perspective and results.

Every day we need reminders that life is bigger than our challenges or our barriers. Daily positive affirmations are powerful in grounding us and keeping us focused on the bigger picture. You can find great affirmation ideas online or create your own positive messages that remind you of your strengths and talents.

It is easy to take offense and attach negative motives to the behaviors of others. Instead of immediately assuming that someone else is intentionally trying to hurt or harm you, change your mindset to consider that something else is happening in their life that is the source of their behavior. It takes conscious effort to change your mindset, but by recognizing that you are attaching negative motives to behavior and then making the decision to assume positive intent, it will become easier to see the goodness in people. We all see the world through our own personal lens which is clouded with our own experiences; remember that other people's lenses are also clouded by what they are experiencing.

Our mind can convince us that we aren't smart enough, experienced enough, or good enough. When we recognize these thoughts, we must consciously stop and replace them with messages that we are intelligent, we can figure things out, and that we are good enough, we have the opportunity to change the way we approach life. What you think about and the messages you tell yourself influence EVERYTHING in your life.

Everything is a thought before it is an action. We all have negative thoughts – the key is to recognize when you have one, and actively choose to change it. Switching your mindset and taking control of your thoughts instead of allowing your thoughts to control you makes all the difference. When your brain tells you that you cannot do something, that you are not good enough, or that you are a failure – consciously knock that thought down with the message that you can triumph!

You have experiences and talents that have gotten you to where you are now and you can succeed. Take control of your thoughts – label those negative thoughts for what they are – **pesky ANTS and squish them with positive counter-thoughts!**

Be careful of the ANTS!

Automatic Negative ThoughtS

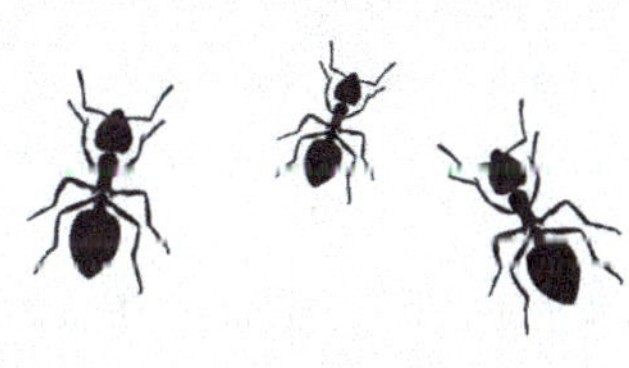

What do you think of when you hear the saying *"less is more"*? – The easier it is to make a decision when you have fewer choices? The more you enjoy a room when it isn't filled with clutter?

While it often seems like the 'more' we get of something, the better it is, the truth is, often 'less' of something allows us to savor, understand, and enjoy it more.

What can you simplify this week, or do less of, or share more concisely?

In my experience, things usually do NOT work out the way we plan. Environmental factors, other humans, and many things outside of our control encroach on our best-made plans.

Instead of frustration or discouragement when things change, look at the disruption as a puzzle to be solved.

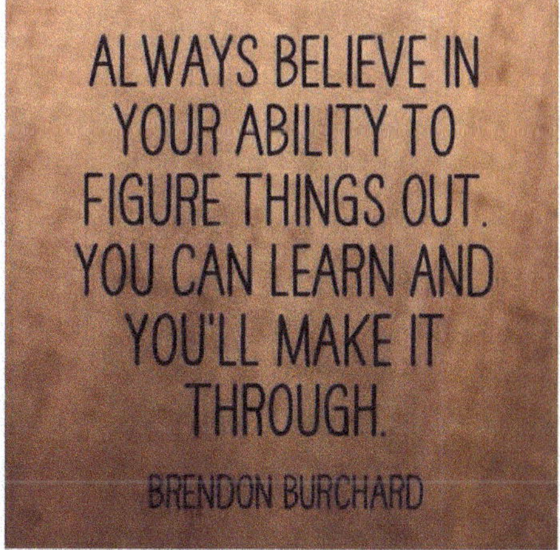

Do you have a mindset of curiosity or certainty? The best learning and growth come when we are curious. Curiosity improves our self-awareness and our connection with others.

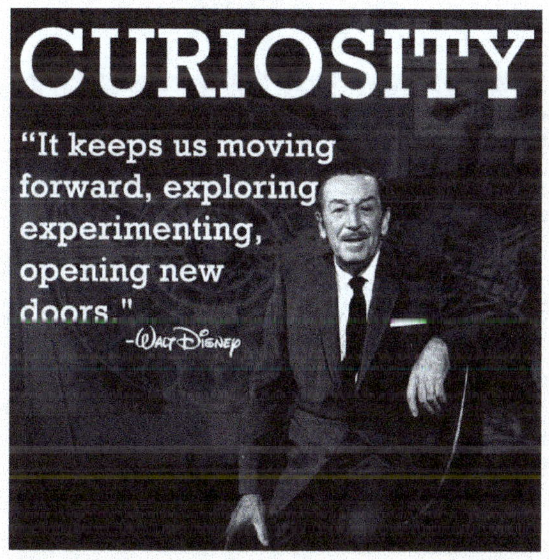

I have found the best way to be curious is to ask questions, listen, research, read, and be open to trying new things and approaches. Instead of being certain of your opinion or position, *how can you be curious and increase understanding this week?*

I hope these thoughts ignited a spark within you, lighting the way toward a future filled with purpose, success, and fulfilment.

Remember, life is an extraordinary adventure, and every moment presents an opportunity to **redefine yourself**. The journey of self-discovery is ongoing, and you don't have to walk this path alone. We all need some direction and support, especially when faced with big decisions and change.

As a dedicated executive coach, I aim to **empower** individuals like you, who might be feeling stuck or uncertain, to **regain control** and stride confidently toward their dreams. Whether you seek clarity in your personal life, desire to achieve unprecedented success in your business endeavours, or simply need that extra push to unlock your full potential, I am here to help.

My coaching goes beyond mere motivation; it's a partnership. We create a customized roadmap for your unique journey. Together, we'll explore your passions, identify your strengths, and address your challenges. You will then be confident to move forward with **practical tools and actionable strategies**.

Your dreams are valid, and you deserve to live a life that aligns with your aspirations. I encourage you to take the next step.

Reach out, book a 30-minute intro call on stephanieschmid.com and **let's embark on this empowering journey together.**

I can't wait to meet you.

Take care,
Stephanie

2023™